I Am An African

**Favourite Africa Poems
By Wayne Visser**

Fifth Edition

Fifth paperback edition published in 2016 by Kaleidoscope Futures, Cambridge, UK.

First and second paperback editions published in 2008 and 2010 by Your P.O.D. Ltd. Third and fourth paperback edition published in 2012 and 2014 by Wayne Visser.

First and second electronic editions published in 2011 by Wayne Visser and in 2016 by Kaleidoscope Futures.

Copyright © 2016 Wayne Visser.

All rights reserved. No part of this publication may be reproduced, stored in a retrieval system, or transmitted, in any form or by any means, electronic, mechanical, photocopying, recording or otherwise, except as permitted by the UK Copyright, Designs and Patents Act 1988, without the prior permission of the publisher.

Cover photography and design by Wayne Visser. Cover photograph by Bob Webzell. Cover photograph of the author by Indira Kartallozi.

Printing and distribution by Lulu.com.

ISBN 978-1-908875-22-8

Dedication

Dedicated to the people of Africa, who never cease to amaze and inspire with their colourful diversity, their warm humanity, their unquenchable hope, their tireless resilience and their indomitable spirit.

Fiction Books by Wayne Visser

I Am An African: Favourite Africa Poems

Wishing Leaves: Favourite Nature Poems

Seize the Day: Favourite Inspirational Poems

String, Donuts, Bubbles and Me: Favourite Philosophical Poems

African Dream: Inspiring Words & Images from the Luminous Continent

Icarus: Favourite Love Poems

Life in Transit: Favourite Travel & Tribute Poems

Non-fiction Books by Wayne Visser

Beyond Reasonable Greed

South Africa: Reasons to Believe

Corporate Citizenship in Africa

Business Frontiers

The A to Z of Corporate Social Responsibility

Making A Difference

Landmarks for Sustainability

The Top 50 Sustainability Books

The World Guide to CSR

The Age of Responsibility

The Quest for Sustainable Business

Corporate Sustainability & Responsibility

CSR 2.0

Disrupting the Future

This is Tomorrow

Sustainable Frontiers

The CSR International Research Compendium

The World Guide to Sustainable Enterprise

About the Author

Wayne Visser was born in Zimbabwe and has lived most of his life in South Africa and the UK. He is a writer, academic, social entrepreneur, professional speaker and amateur artist.

Wayne has a deep love for Africa, its people and its wildlife, which is given voice through this collection. His views on Africa are best summed up in his own words:

> *I am an African*
> *Not because I was born there*
> *But because my heart beats with Africa's*
> *I am an African*
> *Not because my skin is black*
> *But because my mind is engaged by Africa*
> *I am an African*
> *Not because I live on its soil*
> *But because my soul is at home in Africa*

Wayne hosts a blog called Poets of Africa, where poets inspired by the great continent and its people can share their work.

Website: www.waynevisser.com

Email: wayne@waynevisser.com

Contents

I Am An African	1
Africa	4
Wild Africa	6
If These Stones Could Whisper (Robben Island)	10
Lost City of Gold (Mapungubwe)	13
Women of Africa	15
Sahara (Tunisia)	19
Cave of the Gods (Sterkfontein)	20
Little Foot	22
Sangoma in Our Closet	24
A Dragon's Tale (South Africa)	26
Shine, Africa, Shine!	28
Ode to the Elephant	33
Africa Calls to Me	35
First People (Tribute to the San Bushmen)	39
African Dream	42
African Odyssey (Botswana)	45
Baobab: Africa's Tree of Life	47
Where the World Once Began (Egypt)	48
African Time	57
I Know a Place in Africa	59

Africa's Pride (Ghana)	62
I Weep for Africa	65
Place of the Skull (Okavango)	69
Prayer for Africa	71
African Pace	74
Canyon of Mirrors (Namibia)	76
Swahili Spice (Tanzania)	83
Music of Africa	85
African Vine	87
Mandela and De Klerk (South Africa)	88
God Bless Africa	91
African Idea	92
Colours in the Dust (Morocco)	96
Genesis	97
Lagos Lives (Nigeria)	99
We Africans	103
From Whence We Come (South Africa)	110
Africa Proud	113
Free Us To Be Free	116
Africa's Big Five	119
Ancestral Streams	124
Island of Africa (Madagascar)	126
Child of Africa	129
Gathering the Past (Tribute to the	135

Khoikhoi)	
African Untamed	139
Land of the Sun	142
African Renaissance	144

I Am An African

I am an African
Not because I was born there
But because my heart beats with Africa's
I am an African
Not because my skin is black
But because my mind is engaged by Africa
I am an African
Not because I live on its soil
But because my soul is at home in Africa

When Africa weeps for her children
My cheeks are stained with tears
When Africa honours her elders
My head is bowed in respect
When Africa mourns for her victims
My hands are joined in prayer
When Africa celebrates her triumphs
My feet are alive with dancing

I am an African
For her blue skies take my breath away
And my hope for the future is bright
I am an African
For her people greet me as family
And teach me the meaning of community
I am an African
For her wildness quenches my spirit
And brings me closer to the source of life

When the music of Africa beats in the wind
My blood pulses to its rhythm
And I become the essence of sound
When the colours of Africa dazzle in the sun
My senses drink in its rainbow
And I become the palette of nature
When the stories of Africa echo round the fire
My feet walk in its pathways
And I become the footprints of history

I am an African
Because she is the cradle of our birth
And nurtures an ancient wisdom
I am an African
Because she lives in the world's shadow
And bursts with a radiant luminosity
I am an African
Because she is the land of tomorrow
And I recognise her gifts as sacred.

Africa

Gondwana
Born of Pangaea
When separation first began
Like a unicell dividing

Africa
Split from India
And from America parted
Cut adrift and subsiding

Birthplace
Of all humankind
Whose seed has been scattered
Far from the *Ma* tree

Dark space
That light left behind
From progress that mattered
In the quest to be free

Battleground
Of tribe against tribe
Whose rivers of tears
Still bloodstain the sand

Whisper sound
Of fate's changing tide
As hope's rising years
Unify this great land.

Wild Africa

I. Awareness

Africa wakes up, hungry
She prowls in packs and preys
She wakes up wild and wary
And hides in herds to graze

Lurking low, Africa waits
She leaps out with surprise
She sets her traps for bait
And casts her dewy eyes

Africa takes off, soaring
She rides on wings and prayer
She tweets and hoots, imploring
And swoops down from the air

Lying still, Africa blinks
She twitches in her manger
She shuts one eye and thinks
She listens out for danger

II. Renewal

Baking sun and bright blue skies
Tinder sparks to flame
Blazing grass and fearful eyes
Of creatures wild and tame

Thunderbolts and flashing cloud
Torrential rain and flood
Quenching pools and splashing shroud
Roll-playing in the mud

Pitter-drops and patter-sounds
Amidst the mist and showers
Blossom-bursts and splatter-grounds
All painted bright with flowers

Mating calls in season's heat
New playgrounds for the young
Rhyming with new reason's beat
Fun frolics in the sun

III. Diversity

Africa, stretching far and wide
Herds migrate with season's tide
Hippos snort, crocs lie in wait
Most survive, some meet their fate

Africa, living wild and free
Monkeys swing from tree to tree
Warthogs squeal and lions roar
Dolphins leap and eagles soar

Africa, teeming great and small
Lank giraffes and bugs that crawl
Zebras mix with wildebeest
Hyenas laugh while vultures feast

Africa, joining earth and sky
Gorillas nest and springboks fly
Elephants rumble, wise as sages
Life joins life across the ages

IV. Freedom

Rising from the dusty plain
With hope in every burst of rain
This land of everlasting strife
This Africa, our source of life

Breaking out of rusty chains
With wildness flowing in her veins
This land where all creation roam
This Africa, our common home

Reaching out across the years
With echoed genes and veils of tears
This land of skulls and mystery
This Africa, our history

Forever feral, never tamed
With restless destiny unnamed
This land of the eternal child
This Africa, forever wild.

If These Stones Could Whisper

Robben Island, South Africa

If these stones could whisper
What secrets would they tell?
Would it be of aeons past
When all the sky was fiery rain
And lava flowed and rock congealed
To sculpt this coastal plain?
Or would they speak of great divides
When land was rent asunder
By tidal waves and raging winds
And peals of angry thunder?

If these stones could whisper
What things would they recall?
Would it be the first Man's cry
A babe within the cradle
Or infants playing bow and arrow
In hunts that turned to fable?
Would they see a restless child
That set down roots to grow
To write and read, to build and shape
To plant and reap and sow?

If these stones could whisper
What stories would they weave?
Would it be rebellious years
When teen-Man spread his wings
Tempestuous times of selfish pride
Of war and slaves and kings?
Or is the recollection fresh
With recent tragic days
When clashing adult siblings
Each went their separate ways?

If these stones could whisper
What legends would they share?
Would it be of island tales
Of untamed wilds and virgin sand
Or merchants from across the bay
Who scavenged rocks and mined the land?
And what of deformed outcasts
To whom the world was blind
Repelled for their unsightliness
And banished out of mind?

If these stones could whisper
What phantoms would they know?
Would it be of men in cages
Charged with heinous crime
Or heroes of the struggle
Condemned to quarry lime?
And what of tin-pot jailors
Imprisoned by their fiefdom
And all the inmates counting steps
Along their walk to freedom?

If these stones could whisper
What triumph would they shout?
Would it be of dawning days
Where time's great lessons can be learned
A sanctuary, a hope-filled space
Of future visions born and yearned?
The stones echo with silence
Mute with the wisdom of worlds unmet
But if these stones could whisper
They'd say: always forgive, never forget!

Lost City of Gold
Mapungubwe, South Africa

Mapungubwe, rise once more
Up from the south Limpopo shore
Let now your ancient tale be told
Of those who built the Place of Gold

Mapungubwe, on the hill
Your royal tombstones tell us still
Of treasures lost and fortunes made
Before you star-kissed kingdom's fade

Mapungubwe, we can trace
A thousand year old trading base
Exchanging gold and ivory
For spices, silks and rainbow beads

Mapungubwe, let us sing
The praises of your gilded king
Whose golden rhino, staff and bowl
Your riches to this day extol

Mapungubwe, formed to be
A civilised society
And guided by a higher fate
You midwifed our first nation state

Mapungubwe, we proclaim
The untold glories of your name
And to this day your lofty brand
Bestows top honours in this land

Mapungubwe, see it's true
That from your seed a great tree grew
With sturdy roots and fruits sublime
And branches across space and time.

Women of Africa

Women of Africa
In the land of bow and spear
Of chieftain and warrior
Of hunter and hunted
You are the silent gatherer
The unsung provider
The hidden basket
We raise you up
And speak your praise

In the shifting sands of power
You are the pyramid of constancy
Standing firm
Against the fierce winds of time

On the endless plains of possibility
You are the gentle matriarch
Leading the way
Through the fickle seasons of life

In the thirsty dust of desperation
You are the baobab of sustenance
Rooted deep
In the quenching earth of faith

You gather the tears of the world
And in the midst of mourning
You find reason to smile

You gather the tribes of the world
And in the chaos of squabbling
You sow seeds of community

You gather the stories of the world
And in the firelight of remembrance
You keep the spirit burning

Women of Africa
The music of every place
Moves to your swaying hips
And shakes to your stamping feet

Women of Africa
The children of every time
Suckle on your ample bosom
And fall asleep to your lullaby

Women of Africa
The victims of every tragedy
Seek solace in your arms
And find comfort in your voice

You gather the light of the world
And in the darkest caves of evil
You spread your luminescence

You gather the orphans of the world
And in the villages of your heart
You give them a place to call home

You gather the elders of the world
And in the sacred councils of trust
You show us a better way

When our past dries to a trickle
You are the river delta
That reunites our memories
With the sea of history

When our days are drought stricken
You are the tireless pestle
That grinds our hardship
Into the flour of wisdom

When our future lies in shadow
You are the wild prophetess
That divines our destiny
In the pattern of bones

Women of Africa
In a world of folly and fear
Of division and diversion
Of begetting and forgetting
You are the mighty gatherer
The harvester of wholeness
The maker of peace
We honour you this day
And forever more.

Sahara

Tunisia

A silky dust devours the miles ahead
Between the barely living and the dead
The thirsty sun sucks every dewy drop
Up from the bare-ribbed sand dunes' barren crop

Yet strung across the shimmering mirage
A silent camel-beaded entourage
Comes bearing treasured spices, oils and balms
To green oases under shaded palms

Along these trails our history is told
As stories trade and mysteries unfold
Connecting East and West in common cause
And teaching from the book of Nature's laws.

Cave of the Gods

Sterkfontein, South Africa

What is this place?
This home of the stromatolite
Which breathed oxygen into life
When the planet still steamed toxic?

What is this place?
This womb of the mammals
Which found warmth in their blood
When reptiles still ruled the land?

What is this place?
This cradle of the ape-man
Who walked erect on the ground
When the jungles still favoured swinging?

What is this place?
This crucible of the stone-man
Who tamed the wild red flower
When nature still feared incineration?

What is this place?
This forge of the iron-man
Who amplified power in their hands
When the elements still tested survival?

What is this place?
This valley of the ancestors
Who discovered strength in community
When civilization still wanted nurturing?

What is this place?
This tomb of the warriors
Who fought the battle for dignity
When prejudice was still a formidable foe?

What is this place?
This site of world heritage
Which celebrates creation's genesis
When the world still craves rebirth?

What is this place?
This cave of the gods
Who dream humanity into the future
When evolution is still an embryo?

Little Foot

Your footprints in the rock
Supplied a vital clue
A key that might unlock
The mystery of you

They take us on a journey
Back four million years
A branching of the life-tree
When ape-man first appears

Aeons passed in slumber
Left undisturbed by time
Until Man's blast of thunder
Exposed the hollow lime

Even then the shadows hid
In caves of Sterkfontein
The world's first hominid -
Your secret still remained

Until the revelation
By digger Robert Clarke
Brought you commendation
And freedom from the dark

Upon an outstretched arm
Your weary head still rested
And soon your shortened palm
Sparked theories now contested

Your waking in the valley
Takes science to the brink
Could you really be
The fated missing link?

Of you will books be written
Your sleep has turned to fame
Your progeny are smitten
And echo your proud name

Little Foot you have trod
Our path of history
Forever after we are shod
With your humanity.

Sangoma in Our Closet

There's a *sangoma* in our closet
At the office beneath the stair
Most think that she's a little crazy
Taking daily refuge there
They see her through their bias:
The 'girl' who makes us tea
The messenger, the general help -
Why, who else could she be?

There's a *sangoma* in our closet
But no one seems to care
In ignorance they shake their heads
They smile, try not to stare
Their arrogance has blinded them
To her secret, sacred role:
Revered within her community
As a doctor of the soul

There's a *sangoma* in our closet
Whose beliefs we'll never share
Schooled in ancient mystic lore
In magic foul and fair
Around her neck is loosely strung
Symbolic beads and string
An initiate in ways of power -
To dance, divine and sing

There's a *sangoma* in our closet,
A sight both strange and rare
In semi-dark she conjures dreams
And whispers words of prayer
She listens as her ancestors
Give counsel true and wise
She contemplates life's mysteries
Not least her divergent lives.

A Dragon's Tale
South Africa

Breathing smoke, the dragon wakes
Yawning fire, and sighing quakes
Blinking storms, with eyes aglow
Spitting floods of lava flow

With arching back of shifting scales
And clawing hands of fingered shales
With Grabben skin of Trapp basalt
And crevassed frown of geo-fault

Its Lowveld feet and Highveld chest
And Great Escarpment's rising breast
Its Kalahari appetite
And Mountain Kingdom's heady height

Hemmed in by sea, it roams the plains
At Tswaing a footprint still remains
While carcass bones of fossil prey
Still litter mud and Karoo clay

Aeons pass, the dragon sleeps
Dreaming of the hoard it keeps
With gold and diamonds in its plunder
Blissful snores vibrate as thunder.

Shine, Africa, Shine!

I. The Dark Continent

Africa – the dark continent:
So named by explorers
Because the candle of their knowledge
Was feeble and flickering;
Because their ignorance
Was a void of deep space.

Africa – the dark continent:
So named by conquerors
Because the torch of their mission
Was sordid and smoking;
Because their prejudice
Was a cave of grey ghouls.

Africa – the dark continent:
So named by scholars
Because the lamp of their enquiry
Was paltry and passing;
Because their theories
Were coded in white and black.

II. Enemies Of The Sun

Africa is the continent of light,
But there are enemies of the sun:
Despots who snuff out flames,
Gangsters who skulk in alleys
And traders who deal in darkness.

Africa is the continent of light,
But there are crevices of shade:
Valleys where black blood flows,
Corridors where corruption festers
And markets where slavery sells.

Africa is the continent of light,
But there is darkness, it is true:
For every beam casts its shadow,
Every sun has its eclipse
And there is no day without night.

III. The Day of Dawning

Africa's day is dawning,
So let those who talk of shadows
Bring their light to bear;
And those who proclaim darkness
Open their eyes wider.

Africa's day is dawning,
So let those who feed the night
Find themselves cold and hungry;
And those who steal the light
Find themselves alone and imprisoned.

Africa's day is dawning,
So let those who pedal black fear
Discover the beauty of sunrise;
And those who dwell in tunnels
Find their inner flame.

IV. The Land Of Sunshine

Africa is the land of sunshine
Where topaz skies stretch out
From here-now to forever
And each scarlet sunrise
Renews faith, hope and life.

Africa is the hearth of firelight
Where dancing flames leap up
For distant starry dreams
And glowing orange embers
Warm the hands of friendship.

Africa is the pot of rainbows
Where every pregnant storm cloud
Crackles with electricity
And each shroud of grey mist
Shimmers iridescent.

V. *The Shining Continent*

Shine, Africa, shine!
Nourish our shared earth
And feed our common roots;
Green our tree of life
And bear sweet fruits of peace.

Shine, Africa, shine!
Spark our imagination
And confound us with your brilliance;
Flame our deepest desires
And dazzle us with your colours.

Shine, Africa, shine!
Fire our greatest passions
And empower us with your stories;
Blaze brightly on our soul quest
And inspire us with your light.

Ode to the Elephant

Your sacred image looms large
Painted on the rough canvass of Africa
Traced in the shifting sands of imagination
Etched into the hidden caves of the soul

The herd moves as one
Graceful skaters gliding across the shimmering mirage of dusty desert pans
Misty shadows playing hide and seek in the shrouded valley forests
Granite boulders in magical motion over the mottled bushveld plains

You are one of Eden's first-born
Survivor of frozen time
Grown old and wise
Before men learned to crawl

The air trembles in harmonic rapture
As you chant your esoteric song
And the earth shudders in shameful guilt
As you trumpet your just anger

You are the maker of roads
The planter of gardens
And the builder of dams

Your trail of destruction
Is the path of creation
For all that follow in your wake

Death brings sorrow and mourning
Life heralds the joy of cheeky youth
In between, an invisible web of caring is strung
And a sacred maze of kith and kin is trod.

Oh, great icon of this Earth
Memory of our faded past
Conscience of our troubled present
Prophet of our hopeful future
Lead us in your gentle footsteps
On the journey to our greater selves.

Africa Calls to Me

Africa calls to me

With the beat of her drums that mark my days

And the words of her poets that guide my ways

With the crash of the waves that hug her shores

And the sounds of the rain that soak her pores

Africa calls to me

With the tears of mothers that stain her soil

And the laughter of children that ease her toil

With the rattle of guns that pierce her calm

And the bustle of streets that sing her psalm

The sounds of Africa

Are the cries of the world's forgotten child

Taking us back into the womb of creation

The sounds of Africa
Are the songs of the world's untamed wild
Filling our ears with hymns of oblation

The sounds of Africa
Are the screams of the world's disturbing fears
Begging us to embrace transformation

The sounds of Africa
Are the words of the world's neglected seers
Pointing us to the star of salvation

Africa speaks to me
Through the babble of markets on the breeze
And the lament of hawkers so forlorn
Through the heaving of fishers on the seas
And the hoot of taxis at dusk and dawn

Africa speaks to me
Through the roar of lions basking at noon
And the snigger of hyenas in the night
Through the rumble of elephants in tune
And the stir of gorillas out of sight

The sounds of Africa
Are the lashing of slaves that haunt her
      past
And the victory songs of those who are free

The sounds of Africa
Are the crumbling of ways that cannot last
And the hopes for new possibilities

The sounds of Africa
Are the whispers in a din of despair
And the tunes in a maze of lost and found

The sounds of Africa
Are the notes in the symphony we share
And the joy in a land of light and sound

Africa calls to me
With the cry of eagles that frees my soul
And the hush of sand dunes that soothes
      my mind
With the call of loeries that makes me
      whole
And the cicadas drone that blots out time

Africa calls to me

With the crackle of fires that light her skies

And the rustle of leaves that swish her sighs

With the chant of her songs that move my feet

And the pulse of her heart that makes mine beat.

First People

Tribute to the San Bushmen of Southern Africa

First people of this ancient land
Last exiles in the desert sand
To you we owe our destiny
Our struggle to be wild and free

We call you Hunter, Bushmen, San
You sowed the seeds of primal Man
A gentler race we have not known
See how your legacy has grown

For millennia you lived in peace
In harmony with nature's beasts
With tools of sinew, wood and stone
And crafts of egg-shell, quill and bone

Hunting game and digging roots
Tapping trees and plucking fruits
Theatre nights 'round dancing fires
Singing clicks to starry spires

You chose the way of archers' bow
Of hunters' grace - the art of flow:
To give and take and see the whole
To honour life and feed the soul

You felt the weather in your bones
And sensed earth's subtle undertones
You heard the stars whisper 'tsau! tsau!'
And rode the wind, we know not how

The landscape generations trod
Recalls to us your Mantis god
Windswept by myths and scattered tales
And prints revealed on dusty trails

Then came the time of racial blight
A target for both black and white
The hunter turned to hunted prey
Pre-dawning your extinction day

You were the masters of the hunt
But progress left your arrows blunt
And tracking skills that reigned supreme
Are all but lost in history's stream

Yet even now your soul still breathes
On cave walls and in rocky cleaves
In ochre, charcoal, mud and lime
Your images still transcend time

We see your smile in every face
Whose eyes reflect that thirsty place
In wrinkled elders old as earth
Whose wisdom joins us with our birth

First people of this ancient land
If we could only understand
Your honoured ways still hold the key
To setting all our spirits free.

African Dream

My Africa!

As white-hot skies give way to bloodshot red
I breathe a sigh and rest my laden head
As dark descends and blinking stars pierce through
I close my weary eyes and dream of you

I dream a dream of genesis
Of teeming wildlife on the plains
I hear a tale of Eden's bliss
Of sparks of knowledge fanned to flames

I dream a dream of beating drums
Of painted caves and hunters' bow
I hear the voice of ancient ones
Who weave the web of what we know

I dream a dream of exodus
Of journeys over land and sea
I hear the song of restlessness
That swells with longing to be free

I run with cheetahs, graze with deer
I hunt with lions, know no fear
I soar with eagles, hide in dales
I swim with dolphins, sing with whales

I throb with music in the air
I see the swirl of rainbow flair
I feel the stomp of dancing feet
I sweat with fever's tropic heat

I gaze into the firelight
I sit in silence, pure delight
I listen to the elders' words
I rise upon the wings of birds

The rivers are flowing
The brown dust turned to green
The harvests are growing
In my African dream

The fathers are yearning
The mothers' love redeems
The children are learning
In my African dream

The peace-buds are blooming
The hope-streets freshly clean
The love-stalls are booming
In my African dream

As visions fade, all blurred and bled
My world unwinds like loosened thread
As daylight breaks and jet sky turns to blue
I wake refreshed with glorious dreams of
    you

My Africa!

African Odyssey

Botswana

Beneath the boundless African sky –
Unblemished blue overhead
And sun-bleached white on the horizon –
There is an endless African road:
Stretched long and shimmering straight
Tirelessly chasing its own vanishing point

Crossing the vast African bush –
Khaki-clad with stone buttons flashing silver
And mottled coat of green-brown and yellow-red –
There is a rusty African bus:
A melting pot of tenacious travellers
Bubbling with the bright colours of adventure

They find a snaking African river –
A watery ribbon teeming with life
That quenches all who visit its cool shores –
Fraying into a wide African delta:
A floating Eden world
With arms wide open in swampy embrace

En route are remote African towns –
Echoing with fish-eagle cries of freedom
And donkey-plodding hopes for the future –
Nurturing countless African dreams:
Termite-mound aspirations reaching skyward
And ferry-chugging crossings to peace and prosperity

Among them is a wistful African poet –
At home in the bushveld of his birth
And at rest in the sands of the wilderness –
In search of eternal African mysteries:
The eroded ways of ancient flow-lines
And native answers to thirsty questions.

Baobab: Africa's Tree of Life

At the heart of the African plain
Stands an elder strong and sage:
A survivor of sunshine and rain
And mute witness to many an age

But this is no ordinary tree
For her trunk is hollow inside
And hidden unseen she keeps
The secret of her native tribe

For her cave is a place of birth
A haven safe from danger
This womb of Mother Earth
Is Africa's child manger

The Baobab stands proud and strong
She serves her clan as midwife
It's been thus generations long
She's Africa's great Tree of Life.

Where the World Once Began
Egypt

I. Flight of Time

Soaring like a god on wings Isis-blessed
In search of beginnings - a mystical quest
O'er newly wed mountains and islands estranged
'Cross deserts of water - my Horus-eye ranged

In a flash I catch sight of her delta arms wide
She bids me fair welcome, this patchwork clad bride
With gold sand swept hair and brown sun baked tan
I am meeting my maker - where the world once began

II. Cacophony of Cairo

The City Victorious bustles and teems
With the chaos of life near bursting its seams
Hooter blasts mingle with chant-calls to pray -
A whirling sound dervish that's danced every day

The dead and the living find shelter in tombs
The skyline is punctured with crosses and moons
While the tranquil Nile whispers of history unfurled -
The lotus bud blooming of the civilised world

III. Era of Gold

The speaking stones echo down canyons of time ...
The vulture and cobra are shown intertwined
Two crowns worn together - the red and the white
As the kingdoms of upper and lower unite

The floodplains turn fertile and peace fills the sky
From the golden creator, the gods multiply
The sun is discovered in Earth's cavern womb
The word crystallises in temple and tomb

IV. Pyramids of Knowledge

Blocks hewn from stone form steps up to heaven
In praise of the sun - the spirit to leaven
The chambers within are sanctums of peace
Where the body can sleep and the soul find release

Resting content beneath the great shadows three
The lion of wisdom holds life's precious key
Reflecting the dawn on his time honoured face
Weathered with patience - great guardian of grace

V. Monuments of Glory

Amidst all the rubble and ruins of old
Legends still linger and stories are told
Of glory and power, of order and law
Of beautiful cities and triumphs of war

The towering pylons conceal a great hall
Where a petrified forest of papyrus stands tall
Obelisks and statues rise regal with pride
Protecting the family of gods safe inside

VI. Valley of Kings

The dusty white mountains and valleys converse
In whispers of secrets hid under the earth
Of tunnels and treasures and sarcophagi
Of caves where the queens and the kings came to die

The tombs tell their stories in rainbow relief
Of ochre and kohl, green, blue and gold leaf
The walls speak of journeys from this world to nether
Of Judgement that weighs each heart against a feather

VII. River of Life

Tufted green palm trees cling to the shores
Barely escaping the desert's hot claws
Farmers and fishermen battle the haze
Beneath the envious eyes of the limestone cliffs' gaze

On the blissful blue water drift swans graced in white -
The sails of *felukas* shine billowing bright
The Nile's ebb and flow are now slaves to the sluice
As the people and river search hard for a truce

VIII. Legacy of Ramses II

For three generations he ruled from the throne
Constructing and carving his likeness in stone
From statues colossi, his praise song still rings -
The original Gulliver, a giant among kings

Still awesome the sight, though millennia have passed:
The mountain of worship whose face is unmasked
Where horses and chariots do battle for kings
Beneath the protection of the gods' outstretched wings

IX. Vision of Rebirth

Centuries trickle, as the future is frayed
Kingdoms erode and dynasties fade
The sacred ankh's buried beneath aeons of sand
Its destiny resting in time's patient hands

But the soul winds are changing, a gold sun's on the rise
The snake is uncoiling, the bird again flies
From death, life takes breath, we feel the birth pang
And emerge recreated - from where the world once began.

African Time

I'm living my days in African time
I'm walking the ways of season and rhyme
I'm weaving the maze of culture and crime
I'm soaking the rays of scattered sunshine

> You think that I'm slow
> You think that I'm lazy
> You think I don't know
> You think that I'm crazy

But I'm beating my drum to African time
I'm hearing the hum of friends on the line
I'm counting the sum of blessings I find
I'm tracing the crumbs of love left behind

> You think that I'm late
> You think that I'm aimless
> You think I don't rate
> You think that I'm nameless

Still I'm setting my pace to African time
My life's not a race for the clock or bell chime
I'm moving with grace on a mission sublime
I'm claiming back space for African time.

I Know a Place in Africa

I know a place in Africa
Where I can feel the sun on my back
And the sand between my barefoot toes
Where I can hear the gulls on the breeze
And the waves crash on the endless shore

I know a place in Africa
Where the mountains touch the skies of blue
And the valleys shelter vines of green
Where the trees spread out a cloth of mauve
And the bushveld wears a coat of beige

I know a place in Africa
Where I can hear the voice of thunder gods
And watch their lightening spears thrown to earth
Where I can breathe the scent of rain clouds
And taste the sweet dew of dusty drops

This is the place of wildness
Of evolution and dinosaurs
Where life began and mankind first rose
Of living fossils and elephants
Where lions roar and springbok herds leap

This is the place of struggle
Of desert plains and thorn trees
Where pathways end and hunters see signs
Of horizons and frontiers
Where journeys start and sunsets bleed red

This is the place of freedom
Of exploration and pioneers
Where darkness loomed and light saw us through
Of living legends and miracles
Where daybreak came and hope now shines bright

My heart is at home in Africa
Where the sound of drums beat in my chest
And the songs of time ring in my ears
Where the rainbow mist glows in my eyes
And the smiles of friends make me welcome

My mind is at ease in Africa
Where the people still live close to the soil
And the seasons mark my changing moods
Where the markets hustle with trading
And creation keeps its own slow time

My soul is at peace in Africa
For her streams bring lifeblood to my veins
And her winds bring healing to my dreams
For when the tale of this land is told
Her destiny and mine are as one.

Africa's Pride
Ghana

Basking in the welcome
Walking in the rain
Soaking up the sunshine
Gazing on the plain

> Port of slaves
> Place of gold
> Seeds of youth
> Roots of old

Markets on the pavement
Traders on the street
Worship under treetops
Beggars' twisted feet

> Forts be cursed
> Ships of yoke
> Lakes of thirst
> Chains be broke

Motor shops where JESUS SAVES
Banks where GOD'S AT REST
Mini-Mart's where MARY PRAYS -
Retail's heaven blessed

> Grazing goats
> Cows in pens
> Roaming dogs
> Free range hens

Bridges in the forest
Primates shy and rare
Anthills in the village
Bird songs on the air

> Plates of rice
> Laced with salt
> Blends of spice
> Brews of malt

Fashion on the sidewalk
Music in the heat
Gridlock on the roadway
Dancing to the beat

Adinkra signs
Ashanti kings
Changing times
Freedom's wings

Looking to the future
Seeing hope-filled eyes
Sensing newfound vision
In Africa's deep pride.

I Weep for Africa

I weep for Africa –
And my tears water the ground
Where the tree of life first took hold
And its severed roots still spread wide

I weep for Africa –
And my tears salt the wounds
Where the battle for freedom first was fought
And its fallen heroes still lie scattered

I weep for Africa –
And my tears mark the stain
Where the blackness of slavery left its trail
And the rust of chains still bleed red

I weep for the invisible:
For all those who still live in darkness
Because the light of the world's media is dim
And poverty's face does not sell

I weep for the forgotten:
For all those who died nameless
Because the eye of the world's memory is blind
And history only remembers the conquerors

I weep for the ignored:
For all those who cry out in vain
Because the ear of the world's commerce is deaf
And free trade is freedom for the few

I weep for Africa –
Whose mountains are scarred by greed
And whose deltas are slick with corruption
Because power is like cancer

I weep for Africa -
Whose valleys are lined with graves
And whose rivers flow with blood
Because revenge feeds on itself

I weep for Africa –
Whose villages are skeletons of mud
And whose cities are phantoms of dust
Because progress leaves many homeless

I weep for the mothers:
For all those who cradle sickness
Because their compassion does not pay
And life still has a price tag

I weep for the fathers:
For all those who sweat for food
Because the forges of industry are infernal
And labour is still just a commodity

I weep for the children:
For all those who grow up too soon
Because the killer virus reaps a bitter harvest
And childhood is still a luxury

I weep for Africa –
But not tears of pity
For this is a land of countless assets
And a people of abundant resourcefulness

I weep for Africa –
But not tears of despair
For this is a land of vast potential
And a people of inextinguishable hope

I weep for Africa –
But not tears of judgement
For this is a place with its own destiny
And a people whose sun is on the rise

Yet for my forgetting of her ancient ways
And my ignorance of her hidden secrets
For my deafness to her fireside stories
Africa weeps for me too

And for my dwelling in her shadows past
And my cutting loose her community ties
For my arrogance looking from the outside in
Africa weeps for me too

Yes, for turning my back on her wild spirit
And bleaching the arc of her rainbow vision
For my veil of salty tears shed for her
Africa weeps for me too.

Place of the Skull

Okavango, Botswana

In this sacred place
Where kindred still roam
And rivers embrace
Your ancestral home
Once you were king
Over all that you saw
From the dry dusty plains
To the wet muddy shore

Now you are silent
Your head on the sand
The guardian of pilgrims
Who visit your land
Yet still you awake
'Round the campfire at night
When the flames kiss your face
And your eyes dance with light

Then you speak to the shadows
Of the wisdom of ages
Of the secrets of wildness
And the passion that rages
In this home of the spirit
In this circle of stones
We are blessed by the gift
Of your skull and crossbones.

Prayer for Africa

Dear God
For the love of Africa
Hear my prayer

Africa is the cradle of your creation
Therefore, grant me patience
To nurture growth and goodness
In this great land

Africa is the rainbow of your heavens
Therefore, grant me tolerance
To celebrate difference and diversity
Across this wide continent

Africa is the drumbeat of your heart
Therefore, grant me courage
To offer comfort and compassion
In the face of her people's trials

To the prisons of poverty in Africa
Let me bring the liberation of choice
And to the deserts of her suffering
Cool streams of relief

To the tunnels of deception in Africa
Let me bring lamps of truth
And to the jungles of her conflict
Flags of reconciliation

To the caves of despair in Africa
Let me bring voices of hope
And to the swamps of her fear
Whispers of comfort

Wherever Africa teaches her children
Share the lessons of my fading past
And where she dreams of tomorrow
Set my feet on the path of progress

Wherever Africa raises her leaders
Judge my support by democracy's voice
And where she breathes in community
Join my breath with inspiration

Wherever Africa cherishes her wilderness
Mark my celebration of nature's bounty
And where she cares for her people
Watch my spirit swell with love

For the love of Africa
Hear my prayer
Dear God.

African Pace

Far from the cities
And far from the streets
Far from the people
Is where my heart beats
It beats in slow time
In the vast open space
It beats out the rhyme
Of an African pace

With the sun baking down
And the buzz of blue flies
With chirping cicadas
And gentle breeze sighs
There's no need to rush
No deadlines to chase
Just the slow steady pulse
Of an African pace

The cool of the morning
The heat of high noon
The balm of the sunset
The silk of the moon
The stars' steady march
The rivers' etched face
The life loving rhythm
Of an African pace.

Canyon of Mirrors

Fish River Canyon, Namibia

I. Stop the Clocks

We descend through aeons
Layer by layer
Swallowed by the ancient snake
Wandering along the arteries of our thirsty Mother

Stop the impatient clocks!
Enter into geological time
Strip off the manic masks of civilization
Step into soul land

Invisible life weaves the fabric of our path
Footprints upon dusty spoor
Clawed and cloven

Scorching sun
Refreshing river
Rest brings relief to muscles strained
Untrained

A symphony of silence settles
A veil of red rays ushers in the bride of darkness
Her black dress laced with sequin stars
Her shadowed neck hung with lunar pendant

We dance into our dreams ...
And awake to a new world

II. We Are Alive

We winch ourselves out of cosy cocoons
Creaking with rusted joints and aching limbs
Until motion oils and massages us forward
On our wilful march

Slipping and sliding
Splashing and crashing
Stumbling and tumbling ...

We bruise
We bleed
And know we are alive

Across shimmering stone and shifting sand
Beneath searing sun and crumbling cliff

Through the barren bad-lands
The sombre sad-lands
The curséd mad-lands!

Every drop of energy sucked and sapped
'Til at last we call a halt

The swallows dip and dive
The fish eagle cries
We have survived!

The fire licks our wounds

III. That Sinking Feeling

Scenery blurs beneath the unforgiving blaze

Quicksand tugs at our ankles
Rock shards stab at our feet
The elusive horizon taunts us
The eternal "why" haunts us

A regal heron and nervous hare take flight
Bright, cheerful flowers bloom
Where there seems no right to life

The desert erupts into a gushing waterfall
Flowing down to majestic pools and through intricate channels
With the fluid hand of a master sculptor
Inviting respite from pain and progress
The icy river injects life back into our numb senses

The sun bows out to thunderous riverine applause

IV. A Promise of Out

Over the hump and into the canyon funnel
As sentry baboons bark: Intruder alert!
Klipspringers glide across the ragged stage like graceful ballerinas -
The wasteland blues are behind

Our ephemeral thoughts and mood are lighter
But our feet must still plod painfully onward
Through unforgiving terrain
Every step a burden of weight and pressure

Spiral etchings on the jet-black plastic rockscape
Hint at travellers gone before
Perhaps ancient

A pair of fish eagles ride the thermals
With mocking grace and ease
At peace with land, water, sky

The watchful crags let slip their eroded disguise …
Sphinx, tusker, leopard, ape …
Then shimmy back to inanimate rock once more

At last, the distant peninsular summit
Explodes into expectant view:
Home on the rise
A promise of out

V. The Final Ascent

We rise early
Teetering on the fragile cusp between night and day
With finishing fever pulsing in our veins

The towering landscape flows beneath our eager tread
As we succumb to the magnetic pull of civilisation
Amidst vivid visions of all that is familiar and comfortable

Human prints and scattered litter show the way
The gift of orange seems heaven sent
Our turbo fuel for the final ascent

Step by step, we drum
The slow, steady rhythm of the climb
Driven by an unquenchable inner fount
Of strength and hope

Peering faces over the ledge
Are all the reassurance we need
To soar on chill-wind and chain
And clasp our holy grail

We are done
We have endured

Taking our old life back
Is our just reward

Yet after the canyon of mirrors
We see through new eyes.

Swahili Spice
Tanzania

Jambo!
Greetings from Dar es Salaam:
Eternal harbour of peace ...

>Dusty roads and diesel fumes
>Pungent fish and fragrant blooms

>>Cauldron markets, bubbling trade
>>Vibrant fabrics, crafts handmade

Karibu!
Welcome in Zanzibar:
Exotic island of spice ...

>Azure skies and brooding clouds
>Baking sun and thunder shrouds

>>Coastal mangroves, palm-lined shores
>>Exotic spices, wood-carved doors

Rafiki!
Friend of Africa:
Continent of passion ...

> Shaking tops and swaying hips
> Clapping hands and whistling lips

>> Frothing rhythms, stamping feet
>> Pulsing music, living beat

Kwaheri!
Farewell to Bagamoyo:
Place of crushed hearts ...

> Ancient merchants, trading routes
> Bartered treasures, plundered loots

>> Faded portraits, shadowed past
>> Rusted shackles, free at last.

Music of Africa

Music is the heartbeat of Africa
And as we drum
So we are drummed
By the pulse of Africa

We celebrate
As we stamp our feet
We celebrate
As we join the beat
The beat for Africa

Music is the harmony of Africa
And as we sing
So we are sung
By the melody of Africa

We celebrate
As we sing our song
We celebrate
As we hum along
We hum for Africa

Music is the glue of Africa
And as we bind
So we are bound
By the unity of Africa

We celebrate
As we join our hands
We celebrate
As we link our lands
We link for Africa

Music is the movement of Africa
And as we move
So we are moved
By the life of Africa

We celebrate
As we band for Africa
We celebrate
As we stand for Africa
We stand for Africa.

African Vine

The roots of Africa are deep
Her branches spread wide and low
Her fruits are bitter-sweet
She is the vine on which we grow.

Mandela and De Klerk
South Africa

Divergent paths by twists of fate
Ordained to meet, then separate
High branches grown from different stems
That intertwined to make amends

Who are these sons of destiny
That changed the course of history?
Who are these dons of liberty
That led their people to be free?

Mandela – from the Themba clan
Among the hills of Transkei land –
Was schooled to be a royal chief
But chose instead the golden Reef

De Klerk – of Afrikaaner stock
That staked their claim to Transvaal's rock –
Was steeped in National Party depths
And followed in his father's steps

Both knocked upon unopened doors
Both tipped the scales of unjust laws
And each was raised to lofty heights
By willing hands and vexing plights

Mandela – asked to fight the ground
Where dignity was beaten down
De Klerk – compelled to guard the fort
Of privilege that the past had bought

The stage was set for black and white
To go to war or lose the fight
There was no neutral ground to stand
Each corner backed their leading man

Mandela raised the nation's spear
The State replied midst rising fear
The 'Pimpernel' was put on trial
And banished to the Cape's bleak isle

For twenty seven years and more
The battle raged upon the shore
Until De Klerk set Nelson free
To take their place in history

Negotiations followed swift
To heal the wounds and mend the rift
And even while blood soaked the ground
A partnership was sought and found

Until the day – that happy dawn –
A rainbow nation's dream was born
We owe a debt of thanks and praise
To those who led us through the maze

Mandela brought great unity
And showed that truth can set us free
His lack of spite inspires us still
To strive to serve a higher will

De Klerk's great gift was letting go
And having faith that trust can grow
He showed that change is like a seed
That knows no bounds of race or creed

And so we raise our voice and say:
We celebrate upon this day
Two heroes of democracy
Who rescued our humanity.

God Bless Africa

God bless Africa
For she is the seed of humanity
And I am the future through her

When her roots sprout, I am born
And as her leaves unfurl, I grow
When her branches spread, I learn
And as her flowers bud, I bloom

God bless Africa
For she is the fire of creation
And I am transformed through her

When her problems loom, I am challenged
And when her solutions hide, I search
As her suffering inflames, I burn
And as her fever subsides, I rejuvenate.

African Idea

Africa wakes –
It boils and bubbles
It stews and steams
Swathed and swaddled
In wisps of melting mists
And the feathered blue skies
Of my inner eyes

This Africa –
Drenched in sun and sorrow
Stretched in time and place
Bridging north and south
Cleaving tribe from tribe
Birthing a prodigal progeny –
Alive in my mind

Africa moves –
It spawns and spews
It morphs and multiplies
Enhanced and entangled
In human chains of need greed
And white lightning webs
Of synapses firing

This Africa –
Shadowed in war and want
Bursting with light and longing
Dancing dust clouds around fires
Beating drum songs of desires
Endlessly en-route –
On my famished road

Africa sleeps –
It drifts and disperses
It seeds and suckles
Soothed and silent
In fields of ripening toil
And the wandering blotch-herds
Of scattered thoughts

This Africa –
Whispered in myths and mysteries
Cradling its loves and losses
Chanting with hope and defiance
Hawking praise and prophecy
Woven in patchwork tales –
Echoed in my prose

But is Africa real?
This Africa of mind and magic
This Africa of dreams and dust
This luminous continent
Glowing in the dark interior
Of my gold-threaded caves –
This Africa of my psyche

Is Africa fact?
This Africa of books and bards
This Africa of fables and fiction
This luscious land mass
Teeming with the wild life
Of my untamed frontiers –
This Africa of my stories

Is Africa true?
This Africa of tongue and touch
This Africa of nose and noise
This muddled melting pot
Spicing the pallid palette
Of my doldrum days –
This Africa of my senses

Yes! Africa lives –
Africa breathes and beats and blooms
Africa strives and thrives and jives
Africa shakes and aches and breaks
Africa weeps and rises and leaps
Africa sings and soars on the wings
Of my imagination

This is *Africa*
This is *my* Africa
This is my Africa *imagined*
This is my *imaginary* Africa
This is my *image* of Africa
This is my *idea* of Africa
This is my *African idea.*

Colours in the Dust

Morocco

I leave behind the dusty brown
Of narrow streets and sun-fired clay
Back home to England's verdant town
Of scholars' spires and skies of grey

I leave behind the market maze
Where every hue is stacked and strung
And count the march of Christmas days
In gleaming malls with carols sung

I leave behind the emerald bliss
Of gardens in the golden sand
And smile to see the blooms I miss
Still traced upon my lover's hand

I leave behind the hooded eyes
Of faces drawn like timeless maps
And brush the mask of my disguise
With bright new paint across the cracks.

Genesis

Out of the void of anticipation
Out of the time before time began
Out of the fire that sparked creation
Out of the earth that rooted a clan

> Africa swirled
> Africa spun
> Africa world
> Africa one

Out of the lava of molten streams
Out of the swamps of fetid earth
Out of the semiotic dreams
Out of the soils of fecund birth

> Africa rose
> Africa spread
> Africa chose
> Africa bled

From frothing seas and putrid ponds
With plankton tide and Pisces spawn
Life bloomed and bred and burst with fronds
And oceans glowed with Darwin's dawn

> Africa yawned
> Africa breathed
> Africa formed
> Africa seethed

From fertile plains and sandy shores
Some creatures crept and leapt to flight
With fleeting flanks and razor claws
While others learned to walk upright.

Lagos Lives

Lagos, Nigeria

Lagos lives
Seeding and sprawling
Steaming and smoking
Grasping at the shoreline
Gasping at the skyline
Clinging to its oil-slicked ropes
And singing of its toil-stripped hopes

Praise be!
To the God who sets His people free
To the fiery preacher on TV
To the Sunday throng that still believe
Praise be!
To the beggar and the banker
To the fisher and the swanker
To the struggler and the smuggler
Praise be!

Lagos breathes
Coughing and crooning
Swaggering and swooning
Shouting at the winners
Flouting all the sinners
Unleashing hope with soaring psalms
And greasing all the outstretched palms

Praise be!
To the Son who died upon the tree
To the light that makes the blind to see
To the ear that hears each prayerful plea
Praise be!
To the leaders and the bleeders
To the hackers and the slackers
To the hopers and the jokers
Praise be!

Lagos moves
Churning and chugging
Squirming and slugging
Jamming on the highways
Cramming in the byways
Convulsing to the market mob
And pulsing to the Fela throb

Praise be!
To the Ghost who lit the flame in thee
To the Word of heavenly decree
To the Three in One and One in Three
Praise be!
To the movers and the shakers
To the moguls and the fakers
To the dealers and the healers
Praise be!

Lagos lives
And breathes
And moves
To a rhythm of its own
To an ancient mystic poem
To a purpose yet unknown
Lagos moves
And breathes
And lives.

We Africans

We Africans
We, the spark of creation
We, first nation of nations
Remember us
For you flow from our ancestral streams
And your hopes are what mirror our
    dreams

We Africans
We, the crossers of high seas
We, the keepers of memories
Remember us
For you pulse with the blood of our veins
And you cry with the fear of our pains

> We're born, we rise
> We open our eyes
> We crawl, we walk
> We're learning to talk

We Africans

We, the fathers of hungry hands

We, the mothers of thirsty lands

Join with us

For your toil is sweat on our furrowed brow

And your guilt is shame for our here and
    now

We Africans

We, the sons of rusty chains

We, the daughters of dried-up rains

Join with us

For your suffering leaves tears in our eyes

And your great escape is our freedom's rise

> We plant, we reap
>
> We strive, we weep
>
> We serve, we slave
>
> We hope, we brave

We Africans
We, the farmers of the plains
We, the hunters of the rains
Stand with us
For your food is our planted gorge
And your iron is our fiery forge

We Africans
We, the nomads of the sand
We, the stewards of the land
Stand with us
For your drink is our handpicked beans
And your wealth is our tunnelled seams

> We dig, we drill
> We bend our will
> We melt, we mould
> We bleed for gold

We Africans
We, the soldiers of the thorny cross
We, the seekers of the pantheons lost
Rise with us
For your chapels enact our daily
    sacraments
And your deities fill our starry firmaments

We Africans
We, the pilgrims of the crescent moon
We, the students of our earthly swoon
Rise with us
For your mosques echo our calls to prayer
And your mission is our promise to care

>   We kneel, we pray
>   We sing, we slay
>   We lift our pain
>   We praise His name

We Africans
We, the singers of life's sorrow
We, the lovers of tomorrow
Reunite us
For your maps are our patterned mosaic
And your home is our ancient namesake

We Africans
We, the dancers of our freedoms
We, the voices of new seasons
Reunite us
For your culture is our rainbow display
And your genes are our twined DNA

>We drum, we beat
>We stamp our feet
>We weave, we thread
>We love, we wed

We Africans
We, the refugees of futile fighting
We, the tribes of lands uniting
Welcome us
For as you gain so we have lost
And what we give is without cost

We Africans
We, the migrants of opportunity
We, the leaders of the fair and free
Welcome us
For as we join as fragile friends
So we prosper in the end

> We move, we tread
> We search, we spread
> We fit, we fight
> We claim our right

We Africans
We, the archers of the starry sky
We, the askers of the question why
Celebrate with us
For the dawn is strung with morning dew
And our time has come to start anew

We Africans
We, the scatterlings of the rising sun
We, all proud Africans, every one
Celebrate with us
For our future fate is far from done
And we are all Africans, every one.

From Whence We Come
South Africa

Hear the names
From whence we come
Honour the tribes
That make us one

We hear your name –
Venda, Lobedu, Pedi
Ndebele, Kgatla, Ngwato
Tlokwa, Kwena, Hurutshe –
We speak your fame

We hear your name –
Ngwaketse, Thembu, Ndlambe
Ncqika, Gcaleka, Bomvana
Mpondo, Mpondomise, Zizi –
We speak your fame

We hear your name –
Behle, Qwabe, Mthetwa
Ndwandwe, Hlubi, Phuthing
Pulana, Thembe, Swazi –
We speak your fame

We hear your name –
Portugal, Holland, Britain
Malaysia, France, Germany
India, Italy, Middle-East –
We speak your fame

Hear the names
Of our mother tongue
Speak of the words
That make us one

We hear you speak –
Venda, North Sotho, Swazi
South Sotho, Tsonga, Tswana
Ndebele, Xhosa, Zulu –
Your words we keep

We hear you speak –
Afrikaans, Arabic, English
German, Greek, Hebrew,
Hindi, Italian, Portuguese –
Your words we keep

These are the streams
From whence we come
These are the dreams
That make us one.

Africa Proud

I stand upright and tall –
No more bowed back
No more bent knees
I look straight ahead –
No more downcast eyes
No more cowering glances
For I am Africa Proud

See me:
My name is Africa
And I am rising to greet you
I am leading the way
And I am Proud

Extend me your hand –
In friendship, not pity
In peace, not trickery
Send me your prayers –
In communion, not guilt
In hope, not resignation
For I am Africa Proud

Hear me:
My name is Africa
And I am calling to welcome you
I am waiting to embrace you
And I am Proud

I dance wild and free –
No more slave chains
No more puppet strings
I sing loud and strong –
No more lamentation
No more discord
For I am Africa Proud

Feel me:
My name is Africa
And I am drumming to wake you
I am singing to inspire you
And I am Proud

Bring me your gifts –
Of fair trade, not charity
Of respect, not advice
Show me your spirit –
Of community, not greed
Of faith, not fear
For I am Africa Proud

Join me:
My name is Africa
And I am seeding the future
I am shining with beauty
And I am Proud.

Free Us To Be Free

Free us to be free –
Because so much progress
Has been blind to our beauty
Because so much advice
Has been deaf to our song
Because we will only be free
When we take responsibility
For ourselves

Free us to be free –
Because so many leaders
Have been corrupted by power
Because so many followers
Have been weakened by need
Because we will only be free
When we write the history
Of our people

Free us to be free –
Because we are out of sync
With the beat of the world
Because we are out of step
With the march of civilization
Because we will only be free
When we dance the melody
Of our land

Free us to be free –
Because too many problems
Began as gifts from others
Because too many solutions
Have not been home grown
Because we will only be free
When we follow the decree
Of our hearts

So if you really care
As much as you say
Pray, let us go
To find our own way
Free us to be free –
Free to fly the nest of ideology
Free to fight for the dreams
Of our children.

Africa's Big Five

I. Lion

Expectant black to watchful grey
Then bleeding streaks of red

A regal roar to break the day -
The pride has killed and fed
A shaggy mane in silhouette
Content to strut and purr

Across the plains of Africa
The wild and wary stir

II. Giraffe

Pink-purple bruises blotch the sky
Then heal to soothing blue

Green feathered leaves, a long lashed eye
Amidst the thorny dew
An outstretched neck with velvet spots
Intent to reach and browse

Acacia trees of Africa
Extend their welcome boughs

III. Rhinoceros

Fierce-fiery eye of golden white
Looks down with withering gaze

Half-blinded beasts escape the light
Their shapes a shimmering haze
A horn-cursed head dips low to charge -
Vain bid to stay alive

Great sanctuaries of Africa
Fight battles to survive

IV. Buffalo

Puce-pregnant clouds to thunder storm
Then swathes of orange blush

A jostling mass of muscled form -
The knot becomes a crush
A head-flick scoop on spear-sharp horns
Inflicts a fatal blow

Migrating herds of Africa
Maintain the ebb and flow

V. Elephant

Dry-dusty sand to muddy pool
Then slurp and splash and spray

A trumpet squeal of blissful cool -
The herd's come out to play
A flap of ears, a trunk raised high -
It's time to take roll-call

Wild watering holes of Africa
Quench creatures great and small.

Ancestral Streams

South Africa

A drop in the north
A trickle heading south
A stream spreading out
A tide without end
Still the river flows

Nguni of the south
Nurturing the soil
Gathering the herd
Winning the battles
Still the river flows

Venda of the north
Mining the earth
Ruling the mountain
Taming the crocodile
Still the river flows

Tsonga of the east
Trading the goods
Guarding the port
Touching the globe
Still the river flows

Sotho-Tswana of the west
Crafting the stone
Building the cities
Cultivating the leaf
Still the river flows

Lemba of the centre
Smelting the ore
Making the tools
Honouring the Jews
Still the river flows

Ancestral streams
Coursing through our veins
Wellspring of our nation
Quenching this thirsty land
Still the river flows.

Island of Africa

Madagascar

Memories of Gondwana fade
The ancient world torn apart:
As rock plates and craters
Start shifting; slow-drifting –
And outcasts and misfits
Roll Darwin's loaded dice

Mysteries wait in forest mazes
Riddles lurk in muddled minds:
As creatures and questions
Hang suspended; half-blended –
And sky-roots and theories
Sprout upended; distended

Morning wails with jungle mails
Passed along with echoed songs:
As lemurs and pilgrims
Pay homage; seek forage –
And creepies and crawlies
Wait under wraps; bait traps

Feathered skies grace weathered eyes
Ragged roads bear jagged loads:
As farmers and traders
Nurture shoots; count loots –
And children and chickens
Peck, strut and stray; role-play

Islands calm with ylang-ylang balm
Beaches lure with palm-tree cure:
As vampires and tourists
Suck sleepers; play peepers –
And fishers and wishers
Net dinner; get thinner

Insects tease upon amber seas
Rivers snake into muddy lakes:
As cloud-dew and prayers
Flood green fields; bear yields –
And erosion and corruption
Bleed red sands; stain hands

Visions of Madagascar shine
The light of hopes refracted:
As habits and habitats
Start changing; rearranging –
And guardians and dreamers
Gaze into Attenborough's crystal ball.

Child of Africa

I am a child of Africa –
Young and wild and free
I play on streets of sunny hope
And feed on dusty dreams
I am a child of Africa –
Young and bold and bright
I think a million sparkling thoughts
And wish on shooting stars

I do not want your pity
For I am not a helpless pup
I do not want your charity
For I will thrive at first chance
I do not want your mistrust
For being young is not a crime
I do no want your prejudice
For that is your prison not mine

You will know me
Not by the colour of my skin
But by the spectrum of my ideas
For I am Africa's child
You will know me
Not by the name of my tribe
But by the poetry of my ideals
For I am Africa's child

I may look young
But I am older than you
For I was born at the beginning of time
I may look weak
But I am stronger than you
For I was weaned on the milk of the sun
I may look simple
But I am smarter than you
For I was schooled at the knee of wise elders

You will know me
Not by the poverty of my means
But by the wealth of my ends
For I am Africa's child
You will know me
Not by the shadows of my past
But by the brilliance of my future
For I am Africa's child

I do not want your visions
For I have dreams of my own
I do not want your fears
For I have monsters enough
I do not want your leftovers
For I have freshly baked needs
I do not want your playthings
For I have imagination aplenty

I am a child of Africa -
Young and shy and sweet
I smile to hide my nervous pride
And laugh with crystal joy
I am a child of Africa -
Young and hip and cool
I dance my way to destiny
And rise on wings of change.

African Pilgrimage

I have walked the long trail of history
And arrived at this day: triumphant!
I have worn the dead yoke of oppression
And arrived at this day: free at last!

I hear the rhythm of drums –
Will you join me in my celebration of life?
I see the colours of change –
Will you join me in my vision of hope?

I have sung the ancient song of the stars
And arrived at this time: awestruck!
I have heard the wild call of creation
And arrived at this time: expectant!

I taste the salt-sweet of justice –
Will you join me in my banquet of faith?
I feel the fire of belonging –
Will you join me in my village of love?

I have tracked the fresh footprints of nature
And arrived at this place: one life!
We are joined by the sacred web of our ancestors
And arrive at this place: one tribe!

Gathering the Past

Tribute to the Khoikhoi of Southern Africa

I. Spectre Song

Recall the ghosts
Of GuriQua
Who walked the coasts
Of Helena

Recall the day
Of CochoQua
Who found the bay
Of Saldanha

Recall the place
Of Khoi-Khoi past
With faded face
In shadows cast

Recall the name
Of Adam Kok
And what remains
Of Baster stock

Recall the sound
Of clicking tongue
Whose notes abound
In songs still sung

II. Rich Harvest

Tamer of beasts
Patron of feasts
Guardian of earth
Giver of birth

Tender of sheep
Sower who reaps
Herder of cattle
Farmer who battles

Wearer of thongs
Dancer of songs
Tribes who find-seek
Clans who click-speak

Hunter of roots
Bearer of fruits
Master of whale-traps
Reader of wind-maps

People of chiefs
Reaper of sheafs
Makers of law
Harvest no more

III. Melting Pot

From dry salt lakes
To southwest sands
Their dust-path snakes
Through time-baked lands

They were the first
Pastoralists found
With seed dispersed
On nurturing ground

Left in their wake
Cape beaches are strewn
With clay-moulded shapes
And tools from iron hewn

Cut with the scythe
Of settlers' disease
Fate's bitter tithe
Still haunts the sea-breeze

Those who survive
Reconcile their lot
To mix and thrive
In the melting pot.

Africa Untamed

Africa is wild:
A land untamed
A people unshamed
A life unrestrained
Yet there are those who would tame Africa
Who would break her unbridled spirit
Who would cage her soaring mind
Who would chain her flexing body

Rest assured:
They will fail
Like so many before them
And so many yet to come
For Africa is a savage hunter
Forever hungry for the next kill
Always preying on her weakest
Stained red in tooth and claw

Africa is free:
A land unyoked
A people uncloaked
A life unrevoked

Yet there are those who would prune Africa
Who would neaten her untidy people
Who would lop off her thorny tribes
Who would fortify her porous borders

Be assured:
They will fail
Like countless before them
And countless yet to come
For Africa is a sprawling jungle
Entangled with human tendrils
Locked in a deadly struggle for life
All competing for a place in the sun

Africa is changing:
A land evolving
A people resolving
A life revolving
Yet there are those who would calm Africa
Who would tranquillise her young agitators
Who would defuse her creative tensions
Who would dampen down her wild passions

Remain assured:
They will fail
Like generations before them
And generations yet to come
For Africa is a raging tempest
Howling with dreams and desires
Thundering with anger and pain
Flashing with imagination and inspiration

Africa may be many things –
Wild and free and changing –
But there is one thing Africa is not:
Africa is not for taming.

Land of the Sun

I'll never give up
On this land of the sun
Where the people are many
And the spirit is one

There's a battle that's raging
Of the dark and the light
Which side are you choosing?
Will you stand up and fight?

I'll never turn back
On this place of the bow
Where the long walk to freedom
Has a long way to go

There's a new revolution
Of what's wrong and what's right
Will you question the leaders?
Will you root out the blight?

I'll never let go
Of this home of the wild
Where the beasts roam the plains
And the hope's in a child

There's a struggle unended
Of the days and the nights
Will you be strong together?
Will you rise to great heights?

I'll never give up
On this cradle of life
Where the problems are many
And the future shines bright.

African Renaissance

A single seed, on fertile ground
That's how it all got started
A single seed, nothing profound
No heroes crowned or martyred

The revolution will not come
From barren speeches made on high
The battle will be fought and won
In ghetto streets and fields gone dry

Soon, from this ravaged land will rise
A homestead built on ruins of war
As children celebrate the prize
Of peace that lets their spirit soar

A single seed, that sets down roots
And dreams of swirling colours bright
A single seed, that sends out shoots
And bursts into a world of light

The rising up will not be planned
By men in suits and greasy palms
The sign will flash from hand to hand
On factory floors and peasant farms

Soon, learning and empowering
Will break the chains of slavery
The men will dance and women sing
An end to jails of poverty

One seed becomes a million scattered
Far and wide across the sands
And like a million raindrops splattered
Dust will change to verdant lands

The waking up will not be quiet
As drums beat loud with new decree
The dawning is a glorious riot
Of people marching to be free

Soon, from this cradle, bells will ring
To spread glad tidings round the earth
A brand new story will begin:
This renaissance – a second birth.

www.ingramcontent.com/pod-product-compliance
Lightning Source LLC
Chambersburg PA
CBHW061950070426
42450CB00007BA/1113